THE
IMITAT
OF
CHRIS

THE
IMITATION
OF
CHRIST

THOMAS à KEMPIS

HENDRICKSON
Christian
❦ *Classics*

HENDRICKSON
PUBLISHERS

© 2004 by Hendrickson Publishers
Hendrickson Publishers, Inc.
P.O. Box 3473
Peabody, Massachusetts 01961-3473

ISBN-13: 978-1-56563-815-0
ISBN-10: 1-56563-815-8

Printed in the United States

Third Printing—August 2006

CONTENTS

Preface to the Hendrickson Christian Classics Edition. xiii

Foreword to the Original Edition xix

Book One: Thoughts Helpful in The Life of the Soul 1

    Imitating Christ and Despising All Vanities on Earth 3

    Having a Humble Opinion of Self 4

    The Doctrine of Truth 5

    Prudence in Action 6

    Reading the Holy Scripture 7

    Unbridled Affections 7

    Avoiding False Hope and Pride 8

    Shunning Over-Familiarity 9

    Obedience and Subjection 9

    Avoiding Idle Talk 10

    Acquiring Peace and Zeal for Perfection 10

The Value of Adversity 12

Resisting Temptation 12

Avoiding Rash Judgment 14

Works Done in Charity 15

Bearing with the Faults of Others 15

Monastic Life. 16

The Example Set Us by the Holy Fathers. 17

The Practices of a Good Religious 18

The Love of Solitude and Silence 20

Sorrow of Heart 22

Thoughts on the Misery of Man 24

Thoughts on Death 26

Judgment and the Punishment of Sin 28

Zeal in Amending our Lives 30

Book Two: The Interior Life. 33

Meditation 35

Humility 37

Goodness and Peace in Man. 37

Purity of Mind and Unity of Purpose 38

Ourselves. 39

The Joy of a Good Conscience 40

Loving Jesus Above All Things 41

The Intimate Friendship of Jesus 42

Wanting No Share in Comfort 43

Appreciating God's Grace 46

Few Love the Cross of Jesus. 47

The Royal Road of the Holy Cross 48

The Imitation of Christ,

Book Three: Internal Consolation. 53

The Inward Conversation of Christ with the Faithful Soul. 55

Truth Speaks Inwardly Without the Sound of Words 55

Listen Humbly to the Words of God: Many Do Not Heed Them. . . 56

We Must Walk Before God in Humility and Truth. 58

The Wonderful Effect of Divine Love 60

The Proving of a True Lover 62

Grace Must Be Hidden Under the Mantle of Humility. 63

Self-Abasement in the Sight of God 65

All Things Should Be Referred to God As Their Last End 66

To Despise the World and Serve God is Sweet. 67

The Longings of Our Hearts Must Be Examined and Moderated . . 68

Acquiring Patience in the Fight Against Concupiscence 69

The Obedience of One Humbly Subject
to the Example of Jesus Christ 71

Consider the Hidden Judgments of God
Lest You Become Proud of Your Own Good Deeds. 72

How One Should Feel and Speak on Every Desirable Thing 73

True Comfort Is to Be Sought in God Alone 74

All Our Care Is to Be Placed in God 75

Temporal Sufferings Should Be Borne Patiently,
After the Example of Christ 76

True Patience in Suffering. 77

Confessing Our Weakness in the Miseries of Life 78

Above All Goods and All Gifts, We Must Rest in God 79

Remember the Innumerable Gifts of God 81

Four Things Which Bring Great Peace. 83

Avoiding Curious Inquiry About the Lives of Others 84

The Basis of Firm Peace of Heart and True Progress 85

The Excellence of a Free Mind, Gained Through Prayer
Rather Than By Study 86

Self-Love is the Greatest Hindrance to the Highest Good 87

Strength Against Slander 89

How We Must Call Upon and Bless the Lord
When Trouble Presses 89

The Quest of Divine Help and Confidence in Regaining Grace . . . 90

To Find the Creator, Forsake All Creatures 92

Self-Denial and the Renunciation of Evil Appetites 93

Restlessness of Soul—Directing Our Final Intention
Toward God 94

God is Sweet Above All Things and
in All Things to Those Who Love Him 95

There is No Security From Temptation in This Life 96

The Vain Judgments of Men 97

Pure and Entire Resignation of Self to
Obtain Freedom of Heart 98

The Right Ordering of External Affairs;
Recourse to God in Dangers 99

A Man Should Not Be Unduly Solicitous About His Affairs 100

Man Has No Good in Himself and Can Glory in Nothing 101

Contempt for All Earthly Honor 102

Peace is Not To Be Placed in Men 103

Beware Vain and Worldly Knowledge 104

Do Not Be Concerned About Outward Things 105

All Men Are Not to Be Believed,
for It Is Easy to Err in Speech 105

Trust in God Against Slander 107

Every Trial Must Be Borne for the Sake of Eternal Life 109

The Day of Eternity and the Distresses of This Life 110

The Desire of Eternal Life;
  The Great Rewards Promised to Those Who Struggle 112

How a Desolate Person Ought to
  Commit Himself Into the Hands of God 114

When We Cannot Attain to the Highest,
  We Must Practice the Humble Works 116

A Man Ought Not to Consider Himself Worthy of Consolation,
  But Rather Deserving of Chastisement. 117

God's Grace Is Not Given to the Earthly Minded 118

The Different Motions of Nature and Grace 119

The Corruption of Nature and the Efficacy of Divine Grace 122

We Ought to Deny Ourselves and
  Imitate Christ Through Bearing the Cross 124

A Man Should Not Be Too Downcast When He Falls Into Defects   125

High Matters and the Hidden Judgments of God
  Are Not To Be Scrutinized. 126

All Hope and Trust Are To Be Fixed In God Alone 129

Book Four: An Invitation To Holy Communion 131

The Great Reverence With Which We Should Receive Christ. . . 133

God's Great Goodness and Love
  Is Shown to Man in This Sacrament 136

It Is Profitable to Receive Communion Often. 138

Many Blessings Are Given
  Those Who Receive Communion Worthily 140

The Dignity of the Sacrament and of the Priesthood 142

An Inquiry on the Proper Thing to Do Before Communion. 143

The Examination of Conscience and the Resolution to Amend . . 143

The Offering of Christ on the Cross; Our Offering 145

We Should Offer Ourselves and
    All That We Have to God, Praying for All 146

Do Not Lightly Forego Holy Communion 147

The Body of Christ and Sacred Scripture
    Are Most Necessary to a Faithful Soul 149

The Communicant Should Prepare Himself
    for Christ with Great Care 152

With All Her Heart the Devout Soul Should Desire
    Union with Christ in the Sacrament 153

The Ardent Longing of Devout Men for the Body of Christ. 154

The Grace of Devotion is Acquired Through
    Humility and Self-Denial. 155

We Should Show Our Needs to Christ and Ask His Grace 156

The Burning Love and Strong Desire to Receive Christ 157

Man Should Not Scrutinize This Sacrament
    in Curiosity, But Humbly Imitate Christ
    and Submit Reason to Holy Faith 159